George Washington

History Maker Bios

Candice F. Ransom

Backpack Books • New York

To Shannon, a wonderful editor

Illustrations by Tim Parlin

Text copyright © 2002 by Candice F. Ransom
Illustrations copyright © 2002 by Lerner Publications Company

Backpack Books is an imprint of
Michael Friedman Publishing Group, Inc.

ISBN: 0-7607-2830-5

Manufactured in the United States of America

10 9 8 7 6 5 4 3 2 1

Table of Contents

INTRODUCTION

George Washington has been called the father of his country. Americans have named buildings, monuments, cities, and even a state after him. His face is on the dollar bill.

George never thought he would become so famous. Yet he made history as a patriot who led America's fight for freedom from Great Britain. Later he was elected the first president of the United States of America. George Washington turned out to be the kind of leader his new nation needed.

This is his story.

1 A YOUNG GENTLEMAN

When George Washington was six years old, his family moved to a farm in Virginia. The year was 1738. Virginia was one of the thirteen American colonies, or settlements, ruled by Great Britain.

Unlike many colonial children, George was lucky to be born into a wealthy family. The Washingtons' house at Ferry Farm had six rooms. The family owned more than one hundred farm animals. They had thirteen beds, six pairs of good sheets, a watch, and a sword.

But things changed when George was eleven. His father died.

George's mother, Mary, worried a lot. She wouldn't let George ride his pony to school alone.

George's half brothers, Lawrence and Augustine, had gone to school across the ocean to learn to be gentlemen. But after George's father died, the Washingtons no longer had enough money to send George so far away. So he just went to the schoolhouse across the river.

AN HONEST BOY

A famous story tells how young George chopped down his father's cherry tree with a hatchet. When George's father asked who had done it, George said, "I can't tell a lie, Pa. . . . I did cut it with my hatchet." His father was so happy with the boy's honesty that he didn't punish him. As popular as this story is, it isn't true! A writer named Mason Locke Weems made it up to entertain his readers.

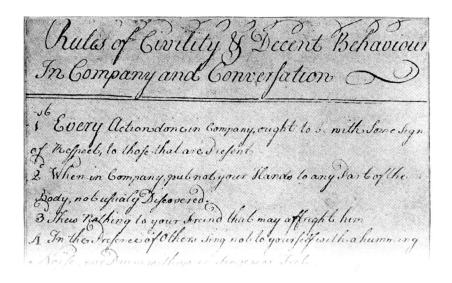

Some of George's rules about manners, in his own handwriting

Even in his simple colonial school, George hoped to learn how to behave like a gentleman. Along with lessons in spelling and math, he copied rules from a book about manners. "Do not kill fleas or lice in front of others," he wrote. "Do not blow your nose at the table. . . . Do not clean your teeth with the tablecloth."

Some rules were more serious. George took note of those as well. "Listen to people when they speak to you," he copied in careful script. "Respect others."

Teenage George towered over most grown men. He was more than six feet tall. He had reddish brown hair and gray-blue eyes. His hands and feet seemed too big. But he was a skilled, graceful horseback rider. And since a gentleman would need to know how to dance at parties, he took dancing lessons, too.

One gentleman George especially admired was his half brother Lawrence. A soldier who told thrilling stories about his adventures in the navy, Lawrence was both well-mannered and brave.

Lawrence Washington commanded one hundred Virginian soldiers in a British war against Spain.

Lawrence Washington named Mount Vernon after Admiral Edward Vernon, his commander in the British navy.

George longed to join the navy himself, but his mother wanted him closer to home. So he went to live at Mount Vernon, a large farm that Lawrence owned. George loved this plantation on the Potomac River. Here he could become the gentleman he hoped to be—and he could learn a trade.

A surveyor's compass used by George Washington

George found a trade to learn one day as he went through his father's belongings. Among them was a set of surveyor's tools. In a large colony like Virginia, farmers needed to have their land surveyed, or measured and mapped. So George became a surveyor. To practice, he measured turnip fields and pine forests around Mount Vernon.

When George was sixteen, he got a job surveying western Virginia. This area was the colony's frontier, wild land where settlers lived in cabins. George had never been there.

One night, he slept on a straw bed that was filled with fleas. He put his clothes back on and lay on the floor. Surveying, he realized, could be both ungentlemanly and uncomfortable.

As George worked, he crossed mountains and streams. He met Native Americans. He studied the land and learned its ways. He liked his work, but he still wanted to be a soldier. Perhaps George hadn't found his real trade quite yet.

Sixteen-year-old George on his first surveying job

2 VIRGINIA SOLDIER

In 1752, George's path changed again. Lawrence died after a terrible illness. The same year, George followed in his half brother's footsteps and became a major in Virginia's army. This army had been formed to protect the colony from Indians and other threats. George was just twenty years old, but already men followed his orders.

Soon he had an important assignment. French traders had built forts in the Ohio Valley. That land belonged to Great Britain, not France. Thanks to his surveying work, George knew the frontier better than anyone else in the army. So he was sent to the Ohio Valley to meet with the French.

George warned the French to leave, but they didn't listen. Great Britain sent troops to fight them. George was impressed with the British army. They wore splendid red coats. They had more guns and cannons than the colonial troops. And they were better trained.

British troops wore bold red uniforms that earned them nicknames like lobsterbacks and redcoats.

Eager to be part of a real army, George joined the British. His knowledge of the land would surely help them fight. But the area's Indians knew the land, too—and they were on the side of the French.

In July 1755, the French and Indians surprised the British in a sudden attack. George was sick and had to fight with pillows tied to his horse's saddle to cushion his sore body. He had two horses shot out from under him. Four bullets passed through his uniform. But he was not hurt.

UNDEFEATABLE GEORGE

A famous story about the July 1755 battle tells how an Indian chief and his warriors shot at George again and again. Not one bullet struck the young officer. The chief became convinced that George could not die in battle. Like the cherry tree tale, this story may not be true, but people still enjoy telling it.

As part of his uniform, George wore a gorget around his neck. This fancy piece of armor was a symbol of authority.

Although George fought as hard as he could, many of the men got scared and ran. The British lost the battle. George realized that they had made mistakes. They had tried to charge, but no army can charge in a forest. They should have shot from behind trees, like the Indians had. And they should never have run away in confusion, but fought back instead.

George had learned some important lessons. If he ever commanded an army, he would do things his own way.

3 MOUNT VERNON

After that difficult battle, George was made a colonel and put in charge of Virginia's army. The French and Indian War went on and on. In 1757, George became ill and went home to Mount Vernon to recover. He saw that while he had been away, his home had become run-down.

George needed money to improve the plantation and to buy more land. And he needed a wife to care for his home.

Martha Custis was a young, pretty widow. She was also one of the wealthiest women in Virginia. George began to visit Martha when he could get time away from the army. They became close friends. Soon George ordered fancy clothes from London. He bought six pairs of shoes and blue velvet to make a suit. He needed new finery to court Martha—and maybe even to wear to a wedding.

Martha Custis's first husband and two of their four children died before she met George.

By the end of 1758, George's troops had pushed the French out of the Ohio Valley. He had done his job well, but he found that the British didn't treat American officers with much respect. He left the army, determined to find a new path.

On January 6, 1759, George and Martha were married. Along with his new wife, George had two new stepchildren. John Parke Custis, age four, was called Jacky. Martha Parke Custis, who was called Patsy, was two years old.

George's marriage to Martha made him a wealthy landowner and a stepfather.

SLAVERY AT MOUNT VERNON

When Martha Washington came to Mount Vernon, she brought one hundred slaves with her. George owned slaves, too. He treated them kindly. Over time, he realized that slavery was wrong. When he died, he left instructions that his slaves should be set free upon Martha's death.

The entire family moved into Mount Vernon. George loved Jacky and Patsy as if they were his own. Now his orders to London included toys, books, and games.

After six years in the army, George was happy to live the life of a gentleman farmer. Every morning, he got up early. He had tea and three hoecakes for breakfast. Then he rode around his land to check on his fields.

Life at Mount Vernon was not all work. The Washingtons went to dinners and balls. In a single year, 1768, George attended two balls, three plays, one horse race, and forty-nine foxhunts.

George also went to meetings of the House of Burgesses in Williamsburg. His neighbors elected him many times to represent them in this group of Virginia lawmakers. Here George learned how the colonial government worked and got to know other lawmakers.

In the House of Burgesses, George found that many people didn't like how Great Britain was ruling them. In the 1760s, new British laws forced Americans to pay high taxes on dishes, paper, tea, tools, and even playing cards. The colonists could make some of their own laws, but they had no voice in the British government. To George and many others, the tax laws seemed unfair.

George's peaceful life was starting to change. In the summer of 1773, Patsy died. And that December, a group of colonists dressed as Indians and boarded British ships in Massachusetts. The men dumped the ships' cargo of tea overboard into Boston Harbor to protest the British tax on this popular drink.

When George read about the Boston Tea Party, he thought the British would respond by making even harsher laws. He was right. The port of Boston was closed, and the city was filled with British soldiers. Many colonists grew angrier than ever.

Colonists disguised as Mohawk Indians dumped 342 chests of tea overboard during the Boston Tea Party.

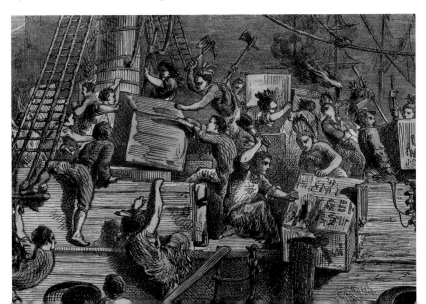

The members of the Continental Congress hoped to work out their differences with Britain's King George III.

Men from twelve colonies came to Philadelphia to discuss the problem in the Continental Congress. George was chosen to represent Virginia.

At the Congress, George listened, and said little. The members decided not to trade with Britain until Boston was freed. George rode back to Mount Vernon, feeling sad. Would it take a war to gain better rights for the colonies?

Soon he saw that it would. In Massachusetts, red-coated British soldiers attacked colonists in April 1775. Farmers and shopkeepers banded together to fight back. Several men died.

The British retreated to Boston. But the redcoats would be back, and they would bring more soldiers.

America needed a real army, not a bunch of untrained farmers. Who would lead them? The members of the Second Continental Congress did not have to look far. They voted for George Washington.

The American soldiers who faced the British in Massachusetts were known as minutemen because they were ready to fight at a minute's notice.

No one was surprised when George was chosen. He was loyal and brave, and he was known for his military experience. Almost every patriot in America wanted to follow him.

George believed the war would probably be impossible to win. The British army was more powerful than the patriots' army in every way. Still, the colonies needed him. He agreed to be the army's commander. He wouldn't even take any money for the job.

Dressed in his blue and buff uniform, General George Washington rode north toward Boston. On the road, messengers told him about a big battle at Bunker Hill. George would have to hurry. The war was not waiting for him.

4 THE FIGHT TO BE FREE

When George arrived in Massachusetts, he was disappointed. His new army didn't have enough guns, blankets, tents, or uniforms. The men were not trained as soldiers. Worse, men from different colonies didn't get along with each other. George knew that only a united army could win the war. He had to make his army bigger and stronger.

Finally, after months of training, George's troops fired on the British. The redcoats left Boston in their ships. George was a hero! He had proven that farmers and fishermen could fight—and that people from different parts of America could work together.

While George and his army fought on the battlefields, Congress decided it was time to tell the world that America was a

free country. Thomas Jefferson was chosen to write the Declaration of Independence.

As commander in chief of the patriots' Continental Army, George wore a blue sash across his chest.

Patriot troops all over America heard the bold words of the Declaration of Independence in July 1776.

On July 4, 1776, Congress voted to accept the declaration. George read it to his men five days later. Everyone cheered. But the patriots knew they wouldn't really be free unless they won the war.

Then the patriots lost the Battle of Long Island. George led his men into New Jersey. The British beat them again. This time the Americans retreated into Pennsylvania. George felt tired. He had not had a day off in a year and a half, but he could not rest. His men began to wonder if he was a good general after all.

George was worried, too. The British still had more troops, ships, and supplies than the patriots. If he took his small army into a major battle, they would surely lose the war. He needed to find a different way to fight.

George remembered his years in the wilderness. During the French and Indian War, the Indians fought from behind rocks and trees. George decided to use the land. He would stay away from cities and make the redcoats fight in the woods and fields.

GEORGE'S ARMY

Many of the soldiers in George's army didn't want to be there once the going got rough. The men usually signed up for only a few months at a time. When their time was up, they'd simply go home, even if there was no one to replace them. Some soldiers got fed up with army life and ran away after just days or weeks.

George's soldiers had to break apart huge chunks of ice to cross the freezing Delaware River.

On Christmas night in 1776, George carried out a daring sneak attack. His men crossed the dark Delaware River in boats. They marched through a snowstorm to Trenton, New Jersey. This city was held by British troops and Hessians, soldiers who worked for the British. The storm kept the enemy indoors. Suddenly the Americans struck! George led his men to victory over the surprised British and Hessians.

The patriots won the next battle, in Princeton. But the British sent more troops and captured Philadelphia in 1777.

George and his men spent that winter at Valley Forge, outside Philadelphia. The American soldiers were at a low point. Their new enemy was hunger. The men made "soup" with burned leaves. They chewed their leather boots. Barefoot, they left bloody tracks in the snow.

About 2,500 American soldiers died during the terrible winter at Valley Forge.

Most of George's soldiers spent the winter in wooden shacks they built themselves. George felt fortunate to live in this brick farmhouse.

For George, conditions weren't quite so grim. He lived in a farmhouse. Martha came from Mount Vernon to run the house so George could take care of the army's needs. He begged Congress for more supplies. Not enough came. So George told some of his men to steal cattle. He sent more soldiers to catch fish. One way or another, he would lead his army through these hard times.

At last spring came and so did good news. The French were still angry at their old enemies, the British. They sent ships, supplies, and soldiers to help the Americans.

French troops joined George's army in watching the British surrender at Yorktown.

The fighting still went on for years. Then George's army began a battle with the British in Yorktown, Virginia. The British were outnumbered. On October 17, 1781, General Charles Cornwallis surrendered. When the British army put down their guns, their band played a sad tune. George realized the song was "The World Turned Upside Down." For the British, who had always been in charge, the world was indeed topsy-turvy.

It took two years for England and the United States to sign a peace treaty. But the Americans won their freedom at last.

Some of George's men felt he should be made king. George thought the idea was ridiculous. He hadn't fought all these years for America to be taken over by kings again.

In December 1783, George said farewell to his officers. Then he climbed on Nelson, his faithful horse, and headed home. He arrived at Mount Vernon on Christmas Eve. He had been at war more than eight years.

GEORGE'S TO DO LIST

BUILD CAPITOL
~~START AN ARMY~~
~~ESTABLISH A TAX SYSTEM~~
~~START A TREASURY~~
FEED THE DOG
~~POST OFFICE~~
~~TREATIES WITH NATIVE AMERICANS~~
PICK UP GROCERIES
~~MORE TREATIES~~
PAINT THE HOUSE
~~NO~~ NO MORE WARS

5 LEADING A NEW NATION

Once more, George traded his uniform for farmer's clothes. But life was not the same at Mount Vernon. Patsy was dead, and Jacky had died in 1781. George and Martha had never had children of their own. But two of Jacky's children lived at Mount Vernon. Nelly and little Washington brought laughter into the house.

Even though George had retired from the army, he couldn't forget that America had problems. The new government was weak. The states acted like separate countries, not parts of one country. By law, Congress could not make them pay taxes or send soldiers for the American army, even if another war began. Would the country hold together?

In May 1787, George went to a meeting in Philadelphia to talk about how to improve America's government. He was chosen to run the meeting.

George enjoyed quiet times at Mount Vernon, but he still worked hard at farming, too.

As usual, he sat quietly and listened. People argued, but George stayed calm. As he had done with his soldiers from different colonies, he helped the members work together.

By the end of the summer, a new document had been written. It was called the Constitution. The Constitution described rules for a stronger government. When Congress made laws, the states would have to follow them. The head of the government would not be a king, but a president.

The Constitution begins with the famous words, "We the people of the United States..."

GEORGE'S SPECIAL DAY

George became president on April 30, 1789, at age fifty-seven. For the occasion, he powdered his hair and wore a brown suit (made in America, of course), silver eagle buttons, a sword, white silk stockings, and size thirteen shoes with silver buckles.

The first president was elected by men from each state called electors. In 1789, every elector voted for George Washington. But George wasn't sure how he felt about becoming president. No one in history had ever held a job exactly like this one. What if he failed?

At fifty-seven, George left home for a new life in New York City, the nation's capital. Thousands of people cheered him along the way. Soon Martha joined him at their home at 3 Cherry Street. Later, the Washingtons moved to Philadelphia. That city would be the nation's capital until a new capital city was built.

George promised to follow America's new Constitution as the first president.

George served as president for four years. Then he was elected to a second term. Being president was not an easy job. So many things were being decided for the first time. How should taxes be paid? How would the country be kept safe?

As always, George worked to keep the peace. He made treaties with Native Americans. He kept the United States out of another war. He helped start a treasury and an army.

He also picked the place for the new capital, which would be named after him. Washington, D.C., would be built along the Potomac River, not far from Mount Vernon.

At the end of his second term, George knew he would be asked to serve a third. But he was tired. Eight years was enough. He wanted to go home.

George gave his last speech, the Farewell Address. Then the Washingtons packed their things. With Martha's parrot and George's dog, they went home to Mount Vernon at last.

TOOTH TALES

George was one of many colonial Americans who had terrible teeth. John Adams, America's second president, said that George lost his real teeth by cracking Brazil nuts with them. At first, George had false teeth made of cow's teeth. Later he had another set made from hippopotamus ivory. They fit poorly and hurt, which may be why he rarely smiles in portraits.

George longed for a quiet life, but he had become more famous than ever. The house was often filled with guests. Artists came to paint his portrait.

George still rose early to ride around his estate. On December 12, 1799, he went riding as always. It began to snow, and then freezing rain started. The next day, George told Martha his throat was sore. He could barely speak. He had trouble breathing and ran a fever.

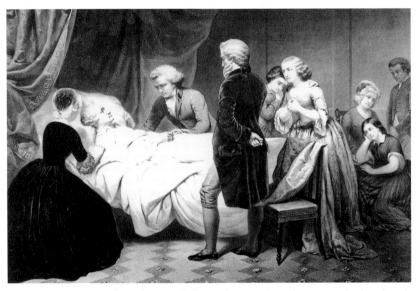

From George's family and friends to the thousands he had never met, Americans found it hard to say good-bye to their beloved leader.

On the morning of December 14, George's doctor, James Craik, came. But there was little Dr. Craik could do. Around midnight, George died quietly. He was sixty-seven years old.

The funeral was simple. Two men dressed in black led George's riderless horse. As George had wished, he was buried at his beloved Mount Vernon.

The nation was sad to lose its great leader. People everywhere dressed in black. In a speech to Congress, Representative Henry Lee said that George Washington was "first in war, first in peace, and first in the hearts of his countrymen."

George Washington was all those things. When America needed a leader of wisdom and courage, he came through again and again. He was truly the father of his country.

TIMELINE

GEORGE WASHINGTON WAS BORN ON FEBRUARY 22, 1732.

In the year . . .

1743   George's father died.   Age 11

1748   he became a surveyor.

1752   his brother Lawrence died.   Age 20
he became an officer in Virginia's army.

1754   he began fighting in the French and Indian War.

1759   he married Martha Custis.
he brought Martha and her two children to Mount Vernon.

1773   the Boston Tea Party took place.

1774   he represented Virginia in the First Continental Congress.

1775   the Revolutionary War began.
he was chosen to command the American   Age 43
army.

1776   his army drove the British out of Boston.
the Declaration of Independence was signed.
he crossed the Delaware River and won a battle at Trenton, New Jersey.

1777   he led his troops through a terrible winter at Valley Forge, Pennsylvania.

1781   he won a huge victory over the British at Yorktown, Virginia.

1783   the Revolutionary War ended.   Age 51

1787   he attended the Constitutional Convention and helped form a new government for the United States.

1789   he was elected the first president of the   Age 57
United States.

1793   he was elected to a second term as president.

1799   he died at Mount Vernon on December 14.   Age 67

44

REMEMBERING GEORGE WASHINGTON

Americans have honored George Washington's memory in many ways since his death in 1799. His face is on the dollar bill and the quarter. Cities and schools have been named for him. Here are some of the most famous places that honor George Washington:

- Washington, the forty-second American state, is named after George. (He appears on Washington's state flag and state seal, too.)

- The American capital, Washington, D.C., is also named after George. He chose the city's site on the Potomac River in 1791.

- His head is carved into the Mount Rushmore National Memorial in South Dakota. The head is 60 feet tall and sits beside those of three other famous presidents: Thomas Jefferson, Theodore Roosevelt, and Abraham Lincoln.

- If that's not tall enough, try the Washington Monument in Washington, D.C. It towers 555 feet high in George's honor.

FURTHER READING

NONFICTION
Collins, Mary. *Mount Vernon.* New York: Children's Press, 1998. A history of George Washington's beloved home, illustrated with photographs and historical prints.

Edwards, Pamela Duncan. *The Boston Tea Party.* East Rutherford, NJ: Penguin Putnam, 2001. A rhythmic retelling of this pivotal event in colonial history, accompanied by illustrations.

Fritz, Jean. *George Washington's Mother.* New York: Grosset & Dunlap, 1992. A humorous biography of Mary Ball Washington, who had an interesting relationship with George and her other children.

January, Brendan. *The Revolutionary War.* New York: Children's Press, 2000. A photo-illustrated overview of the American Revolution.

Moore, Kay. *If You Lived at the Time of the American Revolution.* New York: Scholastic, 1998. Answers questions about what life was like, especially for children, during the Revolutionary War.

FICTION
Peacock, Louise. *Crossing the Delaware: A History in Many Voices.* New York: Atheneum, 2000. Through personal observations, historic texts, and the letters of an imaginary soldier, Peacock tells the story of the famous river crossing.

Roop, Peter and Connie. *Buttons for General Washington.* Minneapolis: Carolrhoda Books, 1986. A fourteen-year-old spy delivers secret messages to General George Washington in this tale based on a true story.

WEBSITES

George Washington's Mount Vernon
<www.mountvernon.org> This detailed site offers a virtual tour of Mount Vernon, photographs of George and Martha's dishes and furniture, and information about their farmland and gardens.

Historic Valley Forge
<www.ushistory.org/valleyforge/> Here's the true story of George's Valley Forge winter, plus details about many of those who spent it with him.

SELECT BIBLIOGRAPHY

Brookhiser, Richard. *Founding Father: Rediscovering George Washington.* New York: Simon and Schuster, 1996.

Dalzell, Robert F., and Lee Baldwin Dalzell. *George Washington's Mount Vernon: At Home in Revolutionary America.* New York: Oxford University Press, 1998.

Fitzpatrick, John C., ed. *George Washington Diaries 1748–1799.* Vols. I–IV. Boston: Houghton Mifflin, 1925.

Freeman, Douglas Southall. *George Washington: A Biography.* Vols. I–VII. New York: Charles Scribner's Sons, 1948–1957.

Lewis, Thomas A. *For King and Country: The Maturing of George Washington.* New York: HarperCollins, 1993.

Rasmussen, William M. S., and Robert S. Tilton. *George Washington: The Man Behind the Myths.* Charlottesville, VA: University Press of Virginia, 1999.

INDEX

Acknowledgments

For photographs and artwork: © CORBIS, p. 4; North Wind Picture Archives, pp. 7, 17, 20, 32, 34, 40; Library of Congress, p. 9; Courtesy of the Mount Vernon Ladies', Association, pp. 10, 12, 28; © James P. Blair/CORBIS, p. 11; © Bettmann/CORBIS, pp. 13, 29, 31; © Historical Picture Archive/CORBIS, p. 15; Library of Congress #USZ62-098589, p. 19; © Independence National Historical Park, p. 22; © Hulton Archive, p. 23; The Historical Society of Pennsylvania, *The Congress Voting Independence,* Robert Edge Pine and/or Edward Savage, Accession Number 1904.1, p. 24; Library of Congress #LC-USZC4-4971, p. 25; © Lee Snider/CORBIS, p. 33; Library of Congress #LC-USZC4-6420, p. 37; © Joseph Sohm, Visions of America/CORBIS, p. 38; Smithsonian Institution, Division of Armed Forces History, neg. #72-978, p. 39; Library of Congress #LCUSZ62-3917, p. 42. Front cover, Library of Congress #LC-USZC4-2968. Back cover, Courtesy of the Mount Vernon Ladies', Association.
For quoted material: p. 8, Weems, Mason Locke. *The Life of George Washington.* Philadelphia: J. B. Lippincott and Co., 1860; p. 9, Moore, Charles, ed. *George Washington's Rules of Civility and Decent Behaviour in Company and Conversation.* Boston: Houghton Mifflin, 1926; p. 43, Rasmussen, William M. S., and Robert S. Tilton. *George Washington: The Man Behind the Myths.* Charlottesville, Virginia: University Press of Virginia, 1999.